Fireflies

FRANK ORMSBY was born in Enniskillen, County Fermanagh, in 1947. He is a graduate and postgraduate of Queen's University, Belfast. He has published three collections of poems: *A Store of Candles* (1977), *A Northern Spring* (1986) and *The Ghost Train* (1995), and was an editor of *The Honest Ulsterman* magazine from 1969 until 1989. Frank Ormsby has edited a number of books and anthologies, including *Poets from the North of Ireland* (1979, 1990), *The Long Embrace: Twentieth Century Irish Love Poems* (1987), *The Collected Poems of John Hewitt* (1991), *A Rage for Order: Poetry of the Northern Ireland Troubles* (1992) and *The Blackbird's Nest: An Anthology of Poetry from Queen's University Belfast* (2006). With Michael Longley, he co-edited John Hewitt's *Selected Poems* in 2007. In 1992 he received the Cultural Traditions Award in memory of John Hewitt and in 2002 the Lawrence O'Shaughnessy Award for Poetry from the University of St Thomas in St Paul, Minnesota. Since 1975 he has been Head of English at the Royal Belfast Academical Institution.

Irish Poetry from Carcanet Press

Eavan Boland, *New Collected Poems*
Moya Cannon, *Carrying the Songs*
Austin Clarke, *Collected Poems*
John F. Deane, *A Little Book of Hours*
Greg Delanty, *Collected Poems 1986-2006*
Padraic Fallon, *A Look in the Mirror and other poems*
Thomas Kinsella, *Selected Poems*
Peter McDonald, *The House of Clay*
Paula Meehan, *Painting Rain*
Sinéad Morrissey, *The State of the Prisons*
Mary O'Malley, *A Perfect V*
Three Irish Poets: Eavan Boland, Paula Meehan and Mary O'Malley,
edited by Eavan Boland

FRANK ORMSBY

Fireflies

Oxford*Poets*

CARCANET

First published in Great Britain in 2009 by

Carcanet Press Limited
Alliance House
Cross Street
Manchester M2 7AQ

The translation of Primo Levi's poem 'Avigliana' from *Ad Ora Incerta* (Garzanti, 2004) is included by kind permission of Garzanti Libri S.p.A., Milan

A CIP catalogue record for this book is available from the British Library

ISBN 978 1 903039 96 0

The publisher acknowledges financial assistance from Arts Council England

Typeset by XL Publishing Services, Tiverton
Printed and bound in England by SRP Ltd, Exeter

for Karen and Helen

Acknowledgements

Acknowledgements are due to the editors of the following periodicals and anthologies, in which some of the poems in this collection first appeared:

The Black Mountain Review, Candle & Mirror, Issue 6, *The Edinburgh Review, The Honest Ulsterman, The Irish Review, The Irish Times, Metre, New Hibernia Review* (USA), *Princeton Library Chronicle* (USA), *The Recorder* (USA), *An Sionnach* (USA), *The Yellow Nib, The Blackbird's Nest: An Anthology of Poetry from Queen's University Belfast* (ed. Frank Ormsby), *A Conversation Piece: Poetry and Art* (ed. Adrian Rice and Angela Reid), *The Living Stream: A Festschrift for Theo Dorgan* (ed. Niamh Morris), *Love Poet, Carpenter: Michael Longley at Seventy* (ed. Robin Robertson), *Peaches and Diesel: Six Irish Poets* (ed. Grigory Khruzhkov, with Russian translations by Anatoly Kudryavitsky), *Something Beginning with P* (ed. Seamus Cashman), *A Trail of Silver Papers* (Shalom House Poetry), *Twentieth Century Irish Poems* (ed. Michael Longley), *Ulster Tatler, Voices and Poetry of Ireland, The Whoseday Book*.

The poems which make up 'After the Japanese' (p. 32) are versions of classical haiku by Issa (1), Bōsha (2 and 7), Bashō (3 and 4), Būson (5 and 6), Chine (8) and Kyōrai (9).

I am particularly grateful to the University of St Thomas, St Paul, Minnesota for the O'Shaughnessy Award for Poetry (2002), and to the Arts Council of Northern Ireland for a General Arts Award (2004).

Contents

PART ONE

Fireflies

The lights come on and stay on under the trees.
Visibly a whole neighbourhood inhabits the dusk,
so punctual and in place it seems to deny
dark its dominion. Nothing will go astray,
the porchlamps promise. Sudden, as though a match
failed to ignite at the foot of the garden, the first squibs
trouble the eye. Impossible not to share
that sportive, abortive, clumsy, where-are-we-now
dalliance with night, such soothing restlessness.
What should we make of fireflies, their quick flare
of promise and disappointment, their throwaway style?
Our heads turn this way and that. We are loath to miss
such jauntiness in nature. Those fugitive selves,
winged and at random! Our flickery might-have-beens
come up from the woods to haunt us! Our yet-to-be
as tentative frolic! What do the fireflies say?
That loneliness made light of becomes at last
convivial singleness? That any antic spark
cruising the void might titillate creation?
And whether they spend themselves, or go to ground,
or drift with their lights out, they have left the gloom,
for as long as our eyes take to absorb such absence,
less than it seemed, as childless and deprived
as Chaos and Old Night. But ruffled too,
as though it unearthed some memory of light
from its long blackout, a hospitable core
fit home for fireflies, brushed by fireflies' wings.

One Looks at One

Gate of Heaven, Valhalla, NY

She steps from behind a tombstone,
is delicately there,
as though shaped from those sad poems
about dead deer.
I'd like her to stand for the soul,
or forgetful beauty,
or whatever lives without fear,

or simply to stop trembling
and accept the caress
of the way I keep my distance,
muffle the trespass
of even a sudden look.
She watches me sideways,
I ogle a Celtic cross

for as long as it takes to be counted incidental,
then not to count. At last I can watch her pass
unscared into the morning, so tuned to place she
is its sole movement. How soft must be the air
in her fine nostrils. How sweet the cemetery grass.

The Kensico Dam

Valhalla, NY

The Kensico Dam is brimming with Catskill rains,
its blocked buttress braced to catch their drift
in valleys cleared years before we were born.
We skirt the edge and imagine the old town
nailed to the bottom, its weathercocks askew
in a climate they never expected;
the past as a windless mainstreet where the doors
mean something different now, the bleached walls
forget what they stood for. Again our lives arrive
at the given minute. Silent, we ask to be spared
the drought that would bare those steeples, release the bells
like alarms-in-waiting. O humour our latest need
for travelled depths and sunlit surfaces,
the random levels won through mile on mile
of serene inland coasting. We stop to breathe
the air off water invisibly awash
with all that has touched it – the crumbling, lived-in rooms,
the earth of mountains dissolved like a rare mineral.
Somewhere under our feet it sifts and falls
towards the future of cities, primed to catch the light
in a lifted glass, freshly as from its cloud,
or flood a sprinkler, purely, for its brisk
spritz in the garden. Right that it should prepare
the flesh for love, then carry out to sea
the sweat of lovers, the loose dirt of our lives
on its next journey. So whatever yearns to be clear,
the part of us that is water, the part that is not,
quickens where water gathers. To cross, we think,
might make the difference, where earth and sky
meet in their long refinement. In this cleansed calm
whatever we wish ourselves seems there for the taking.
So far so good, the silence says from here
to the mountains, its passionate reserve
a tone of the landscape. *So much, so much in store*,
the shore's silent echo. The dam recedes

into our rear-view mirror, takes its place,
with lost fields and woods and city streets,
in reflection-country, the geography of mood
we carry with us. Waiting to be re-formed
in dream and daydream, already it locates
what is richly unfinished, already its shade extends
to the day's next arrivals stepping from cars:
couples and children, under a cloudless sky.

At the Lazy Boy Saloon and Ale Bar

White Plains, NY

The beers of America find their local here,
the Dixie Crimson Voodoo, the Winter Hook,
the Magic Hat Fat Angel. Whole seasons have arrived
in brown bottles from Oregon and Vermont,
Wisconsin and Colorado, to be enjoyed
outdoors while the light holds or at lamplit tables.
We have travelled a hundred beer-miles past the doors
of Nat's, Joe's, Mike's, Pat's, Al's, where tonight
they are serving their full range: Bud and Bud Lite.
Neither beer-snobs nor connoisseurs, we roll the names
like lines from favourite poems: Dundee's Honey Brown,
Victory Golden Monkey, Eye of the Hawk.
God forbid we should try to drink them all,
or sink them alphabetically, state by state,
or yet at random. An early call is best
for Twisted Tea, the Arrogant Stone Bastard.
Then we can relax into Leinenkugel's Honey Weiss.
I sidestep, as before, the Dogfish Head Raison D'Etre,
preferring the sound of Rockford Red Ale
and Old Rasputin. That miner down from the hills
with a thirst the size of parched Namibia,
ready to trade the Newmont Azurite stone
for as much hooch as he can stomach,
would think this heaven. Now, as the late fall
becomes early winter, the Anchor Christmas Ale,
the Wagner Valley Sled Dog, will have their day.
But not just yet. Tonight our one for the road
is the Woodchuck Dark Cider, so that, with luck,
whatever sleep we drift in, miles before dawn,
will be richly human, full of scents and ripe tones
and magnified apples. Its music will be the clink
of lifted bottles. Glasses will tilt to receive
our soul-beer, our personal amber, the wheat of our dreams.

Valhalla Journal

1 Next Stop

The dark tetchy with thunder.
Our upstate train
rushes through midnight.
Out there, invisible,
the cemeteries begin
in unopened ground.
Then obelisks, temple-tombs
on the upper slopes,
as though darkness disinterred
Memphis or Nineveh.
Death as a landscape:
impeccable trees and lawns.
Death as a realtor's dream:
a dormitory town
within reach of the city,
a tasteful settlement
endlessly in demand,
with very quiet neighbours.
Thunder again. Somewhere ahead
the rain-lashed platforms.
Next stop, Valhalla.

2 Cemetery Walks

No doubt you think us
melancholy as moles
in a hamlet where half
the suburbs are cemeteries.
Not so. You too would relish
the sweep of Lakeview, unfenced,
between Kensico and Sharon Gardens,
headstones skirting the tarmac,
charming as squirrels,
on your way to work.

Gate of Heaven
in autumnal mode
would be just your thing,
a park with gravitas.
I see you stop twice
among the browns and ambers,
homage to James Cagney and Babe Ruth.

Today, in Sharon Gardens,
I choose the line
of Minnetonka Brook.
No Styx or Lethe,
open and above ground,
it has never forgotten the sky.
It ushers me down
to river, road, railway,
the travel lines,
their brisk continuum
of starting points
and destinations.
I like to stand
in the one place it dips,
briefly, under the tracks,
then slips out to renew
its old ease with the light,
a fresh current glistening
into the world
of co-ops and condos,
grackles and chickadees,
bee-lines and bottle-banks,
skunks, groundhogs, moles.

3   *In Kensico Cemetery*

Redwinged blackbirds
over Rachmaninov's grave.
Rich darkness,
splash of feather-blood.
Fugitive and freestyle,

suddenly they fan out,
tomb-hopping at random.
Lift into the trees
so easily
that how they disappear
leaves nothing like absence.
Spring has come north.
A minute's silence fills
with the big hands of Rachmaninov
spanning the keys,
the passionate concertos
in which he is alive and well.

4   *After the Storm*

Right away everything subverts
the snow's ambition
to be a deathmask.
The snowploughs are out
between Lakeview and Legion Drive,
winning the ground back
for the day's burials.
At three, the first cortège,
black limousines
with darkened windows,
hushed as though fitted
with silencers.
They draw up at a mound
gouged from the frozen earth
by mechanical diggers.
The trees, at intervals,
release themselves
in slumps and shakings.
And, inaudible, almost invisible,
the hungry birds begin
to sculpt a lost cemetery
from six hundred acres of snow.

5 *Immigrants*

Our histories gather behind us, wherever we are.
Italian nights, Irish nights, Polish nights
at the Dam Plaza, the dam itself
more deeply underground
than it looms in immaculate stone.
The immigrants who built it planned out first
their own village, with hospital and school,
the North White Plains where their descendants settled.
No one alive remembers the laying
of the first stone or the last.
The grandchildren speak English with an accent.
The last off the plane, too, are finding their feet
where the dam waters blend and filter
a hundred streams from the hills.

Stormy Night, Route 87

Lit up like fairground trailers, the tall trucks sway
in the fast lane, festive and dangerous.
We hold to the thruway in illumined rain,
procession of red tail lights funnelling south,
the restless by-notes of a thunderous score
in ghostly lightning. An improvised tattoo
on roof, bonnet, windscreen adumbrates
our role in the percussion, while, like attendant stars,
Sunoco, Amoco, Getty loom and recede,
loom and recede. Is it rash we have no fear,
as swathe after swathe the wipers synchronise
an expected future, its lines, lanes, signposts
clear as we need? Ahead the Tappan Zee Bridge
burns on the water, brash as an all-night mall.
Nerveless, secure, we share its confident leap
between banks of darkness, the storm lantern blur
of towns on the Hudson signalling where we began.
Let shore, home, shelter, whatever we trust
awaits us at journey's end, take wing as a prayer
for the black bear astray from the Catskills, for the deer
with frightened eyes whose ancestors might have gazed,
a century since, untroubled, from a bare
landscape of the Hudson River School.
May they lie low until morning. Let none be found
dead by the roadside or washed up on the shore.
If cross they must, we want them to look both ways,
or, better still, sleep where they stand until
silence awakes them, as it will wake us, to sunlit-
for-a-while, for-a-while-stormless, tomorrows.

Dry Side or Wet Side?

Somebody's dark joke
about suicides at the Dam.
A local flippancy
to put death in its place,
pinpoint and shrug off
the poignance of final choices?
Perhaps we should learn to allow
that tart antithesis,
its heartless-seeming, step-
back-from-the-edge,
snook-cock at whatever
ended there
and how it ended.
Perhaps we should be appalled
such words were uttered,
that we will pass them on
in a trespassy, dry-eyed whisper.
Imagine them grow to outrage
in the ears we would
least like to hear them.
Imagine the bereaved
turning as one
from a dozen gravesides,
their wet faces,
their unanswerable eyes.

Davis Brook

Valhalla, NY

I

In the still hour between trains on the Harlem Line,
in a lull between urgent tyres on the Bronx River Parkway,
in a sudden absence of cars on Broadway, Valhalla,
you may catch its insistent trickle,
the first earth-sound in these parts.

It channels itself down through cemetery fields
to the edge of the tracks, where the builders of roads and rails
have ushered it underground in the hamlet it once named.
Crossing those parallels, it shows again between street and parkway,
well on its way home to the Bronx River.

II

Days when I wait early for the Manhattan train,
the Honda Civic cooling under the trees
in the station car park, often I am at one
with that hatted rambler poised on a mossy stile,
somewhere between frontispiece and scrolled *Finis*
in a book from another century. Its verses hum
with rills and freshets, his head is reverently attuned
to murmurs, gurgles, the little waterfalls
of a reflective music. I imagine him here, like me,
on a July morning, content when the train is late.
Like me, at the platform edge and taking the time,
in the least silence, to listen for Davis Brook.

Washington's Headquarters

White Plains, NY

View by appointment only. Beware ticks.
Something opaque and sidelined on Virginia Road,
a farmhouse without a farm, half-turned away
since the Battle of White Plains. In two days
the Revolution located elsewhere, the house withdrew
into the husk of more than itself.
Around it, for two centuries, the spread and rise
of a suburban city. Virginia Road belongs
to Byram Concrete and Wallaeur's Paint Supply
and Nuway Complete Kitchens. Something contained.
Something preserved and absent. A silent space
where blinds fall and settle, dust-covers brush the floor.
That little dark rodent caught in the act
of going to ground had its back to us from the start.
Too late, too late to fix a silhouette
you could put a name to. No echo to detect
in the empty car park or under the locked door.
The present is a thicket of sound, the dust of industry
a fine web in the trees, an invisible drift
across parkways, the new towers of White Plains.
Whatever haunts the present as the past's
unfinished business, lives endless, as it must,
in the moment we own it, then, as it must, defers
to what the moment offers: the tiniest grey mote
from the cement works, the whole arch of the sky,
where, just now, a small plane is crossing,
the waiting-for-no-one, ceaseless rush and roar
of cars on the Taconic. What dirt-track, what stony lane
dissolves in the foundations? A nameless line
from an old battle-plan sunk in Virginia Road,
untraceable now but taking the weight of the day
in its fourth century. The house is swallowing light.
It sits like an ageing uncle. You half-wish it spared
the long, spectral twilight, the life-support
with dials tuned to 'history' and 'heritage'.

You want it to drift like memory, released at last
from the tug of its moorings, or think of it setting sail,
dawn after dawn, on its one maiden voyage.
You imagine the kitchen table commandeered
for the War of Independence. The big map is unfurled.
Four plain jugs and the General's arms pin it in place.
Those faces at the side window must belong
to Ann and Elijah Miller. When their eyes meet yours,
briefly they have the look of prisoners
in their own dream house, allowed to glimpse, just once,
the trespass of the future. This must be the day
that Washington moved on, the day the Miller place
became Washington's Headquarters. You too skirt the edge
of what you might feel, or sense you ought to feel.
Time now to back away. You back away
until it is time, deferring, to turn your back
on that charged silence. Without missing a beat,
the present forgives you what you almost missed
in your almost-absence. Reclaims you as one of its own.

What Will Survive

We imagine it
because it has happened.

Those who are about to die
are calling their loved ones.

They are bidding even now
for the best words in the best order.

Or on a final stammering run
towards the one word that matters:

the one that may register first
as message missed,

the one that may echo forever
when an answerphone clicks on.

New World

I

As is only natural, you drift to sleep
in the Museum of Natural History,
snore in your buggy under the primate tree,
the evolutionary tree of fishes,
as one exhausted after a long journey.

The African spirit dancer in his costume of snails,
the Chinese child-bride in her wedding-chair
who will step down as woman, you miss for now.
In time we'll tell you about the hermaphrodite fish,
the Unisexual Whiptail Lizard.

II

Awake you miss nothing, have mastered in reverse
the steps to this upstate garden where everything excels
at being seen for the first time.
Here is the cardinal's red stab
renewed in the woodpile, the jay's proud pose
on a neighbour's flagpole, confirming his blue,
and the squirrel's ripple and stop in the long grass
or sudden clawed dash for the top branches,
shattering his personal best.
I love how, wrong-footed by the high
then low jinx of the fireflies among the elms,
you fall over backways but manage to keep an eye
on the main action. Lose track of me where you squat
among sturdy roots, half-visible, half-submerged,
as though set down living, there, from the family tree
to make what you can of its litter, its long shadow.

Two Birthday Poems

1

for Eoin Walden
born 14 January 2005

It is snowing in White Plains the night you are born,
drifts in the hospital car park, a shredded sky
re-forming as open pages along the verge
of the Bronx River Parkway. Trains on the Harlem Line
announce themselves by the hour, rush to define
the lines of their latest journey. Stillness attends
the roof of Washington's Headquarters, battened down
as for a long winter campaign, while further north
there are six cemeteries headstone-deep in snow
in the fields round Valhalla. What a homecoming lies in store
to the house with one light burning and the heating left on.
But now it is snowing, at midnight, in White Plains.
Such beauty transforming the dark. Not two hours old,
you take to the air, at ease with everything.

2

for Conor Walden
born 4 September 2007

In your lifetime
it will be deemed safe
to reopen the road
over the Dam.
When planes cross
you will look up without fear.
That monument in the trees
will gleam all night
from a world before you were born.

You will learn to catch fireflies.
In your cupped hands
they will beat and beat
like little hearts of darkness.
You will free them and give chase
to the one of your choice.
You will follow its lead
into the whole world of fireflies.

Some Older American Poets

Borders Bookstore, White Plains, NY

Tired of the accomplished young men
and the accomplished young women,
their neat cerebral arcs and sphinctral circles,
their impeccable chic, their sudden precocious surge,
their claims to be named front-runner,
I have turned to the ageing poets – the marathon men,
the marathon women – the ones who breasted the tape
and simply ran on, establishing their own distance.
Home after another funeral they walk by the pond
with a sense of trees thinning and cold in the air,
yet thrill to the dog's passionate slapstick,
his candid arse-up in the debris of last year's storms.
You sprightly mortals, you rowdies at death's door,
for whom the last moment is not too late to begin!
I can't get enough of you, bright-eyed and poetry mad
in the fields next to the cemetery, where you drop to your knees
before the first flower in the world, where you lift your heads
to that bare cry among brambles, the original bird.

On Not Hearing the American Nightjar

'Whippoorwill Ridge' on signposts 'Whippoorwill Way',
but the bird itself stayed silent. For all we knew
it had died out, its name and note preserved
as pastoral echo where the turnpike roared.
But no! It was common there, the voice of the place,
sounding the woods at night beyond the last
scraps of porch-light. Maybe we half-heard
when our thoughts were elsewhere.
Maybe it cried when we were not listening.
So often hushed to receive it, we tuned instead
to a great gap in nature. Day after day,
nothing. The indrawn breath
of places touched in passing, their secret withheld.

Catching Fireflies

1 *Fireflies in a Belfast Garden*

Even in winter
I seed our patch of grass
with fireflies from the haiku poets.

Tonight the American firefly
gleams in our hedge
from the poems of Charles Wright.

Mindful of time and place, I think instead
of spent incendiaries and the cautious first
fireworks of celebration,

but notice also, from page to page, the dark stain
of crows and ravens, the patient slow hover
of the yellow-tailed hawk.

Rhythm of horses grazing –
all it takes
to set the fireflies dancing.

Firefly-beads,
a chain of twinkling lights
along the edge of the water.

Firefly-viewing
on the river. That drunken
steersman will drown us all!

How silly of me! Hunting
fireflies in the dark,
I grab a bramble.

In the long night of the heart
I reach out
for a firefly.

Roadside shrine with Buddha.
The firefly
pays his respects.

The fireflies rehearse
the story of their lives –
How they light up and die.

Barely finished sparking,
it is lost in the dark –
the firefly.

Sorrow begins
where its light dies in my hand –
the firefly.

3 *Firefly Hour*

After you, Rufus.
No, after you.
We're fireflies, for God's sake!
Let's improvise.

> Lull between fireflies.
> I trust my friends miss me,
> are counting the days.

Sparks that died in the anvil
reborn at night
on the floor of the ruined forge.

> All my life
> an anxious optimist,
> I wait on the dark porch
> for firefly hour.

4   *The Celtic Firefly*

Exists only in disguise.
Is even harder to track
than his elusive ancestor,
the bogland will o' the wisp.

Here he begins his descent
as a revolving light
on the belly of a night flight
from Tokyo or JFK.

There he has scaled the masts
of a mountain transmitter
to blink at the top,
invisible from five counties.

And here he lives hand to mouth,
hand to mouth,
in the dark yards behind bars
where smokers go
to endure their exile.

PART TWO

The Aluminium Box

It demands to be handled with care,
has a seat to itself on the bus from Enniskillen.
John Wayne is in it and Clint Walker and Joel McCrea
And *Randaloph Scott who never lost his hat,*
Witchita and Dodge City and Boothill.
Strongbox, capsule, payload, portable safe,
with all of us riding shotgun.

A big-arsed countrywoman sits on it once,
reversing in oblivious. We watch her leap
as though bitten by a rattlesnake.
Steve Reeves is in it and Red Buttons and Rip Torn,
its sealed stillness holding the light at bay
between sleepy, no-horse towns.
'Kirk' and 'Burt', we mutter, like bilious frogs.

A couple of nights at the Astral,
two at the Ritz. Next stop the Adelphi.
Marilyn is in it and Gina and Sophia Loren,
the saloon girls of El Paso and Santa Fe
with skirts at the ready.
Open-mouthed, we will yearn through smoky air
for the lips of Kim Novak and Tuesday Weld.

Getting off a mile from the town
is like leaving the stalls before the trailers finish.
'Big crowd on the bus, son?' my mother drawls,
her habitual question.
'It was packed, Maw,' I tell her, 'packed to the door.'

Silent Reading

Like something dark accomplished, or brightness denied
its afternoon flourish, a youthful shadow falls
across rows of pages. Her name is there and gone
in the open-and-shut echoes of
Amsterdam. That name is half my own.

And silence is almost sound, the classroom mined
with casual menace: the creak of old boards,
the lethal whinge of ageing castors.
We won't survive the hour if a pen
rolls at our feet or squat crayon clatters.

The clock's hands edge towards noon. A subtle wind
takes up where it left off beyond the wall
in Tierney's orchard. Unrescuably far,
she fades a day further, yet holds her claim
in every bowed head and moving finger.

A bell completes the morning, the room explodes
in hacks and sneezes. 'Bless you!' the teacher says:
it might be forgiveness as we stand in line
by the main door, our readers handed in
like exit passes. Then dart out to confirm

the air, the orchard, the grass, the concrete, the sky.

The Rabbit

Hangs dead behind the door, hind legs strung
as never in life.
No one has closed its eyes.

Its lips wince back
as though caught in the act
of twitching a ticklish whisker.

What starts as drip
ends as dried splash
on the *Fermanagh Herald*.

More deeply dead by the hour,
it will be sold
to a man in a Morris Minor.

My father will wrap it tenderly
in his jacket
and smuggle it out to the car.

Smiling Foetus

It would seem he has just got the ancestral joke
that cracks the combination,
those fifty-or-so tiny muscles set in gear,
we hope for a lifetime. Already he can do
shit-faced and village idiot and Mr Magoo,
or hang from his ears that helpless hammock-mouth
brought on by women. Perhaps he has learned, besides,
that the womb is a bouncy castle, the umbilical cord
a bungee jumper's dream, or simply hears
those twee, improbable sound waves from outer space
that exhort him to say cheese.
Nothing, as yet, to wipe the smile from his face,
no fear of wrinkles, no myth of original sin.
May his smile turn to laughter. May he laugh till he cries
all the way into the world. May he die laughing.

The Hole in the Roof

Two slates, perhaps, no more.
Yet, nights of storm,
it haunts me sleepless,
gradual and unrepaired.
I think of them looking up
until it becomes
the one thing I have left them,
their gaping hurt
bare now and forever
to the wind and the sky.

Blackbirds, North Circular Road

They were here long before us,
so seem to preside
through our first winter.
Snow in the garden
a chance not to be missed,
they swivel and flit,
as though in time and space
they mapped the neighbourhood:
a random, elliptical print
their work in progress.

This one a Presbyterian,
sleeping rough
in the grounds of Rosemary Church.
The one disposed
to match profiles with Cavehill,
a tunic rag from an old rebellion.
Settling and resettling, a third recalls
the merchant Jew who built here. We share his view
of distant shipyard cranes,
the glint of water.

And this must be the Blackbird of Belfast Lough,
released to the air one summer
from the verge
of a monkish gospel.
Yes, this will be Yellow Bill
on the latest leg of his journey, fluttering down
yards from the study window,
bringing us the free
gift of his ease in the barbed winter hedges,
his nonchalant, deft slalom in the snowbound tree.

from *City Journal*

1 *Aubade*

Last week Bashō,
this week Galway Kinnell
in the poetry pocket
of my black overcoat.
I carry them next to my heart
on the Carr's Glen bus,
the No. 61, via Cavehill Road.
When the blind woman boards
I lift my eyes
to admire her stick-work.
How uncannily she knows
exactly where to step off.
In Royal Avenue
I accept a tract
about Death or Eternity
or the Wages of Sin.
Meanwhile, jobless immigrants
are bending the law
at every traffic light,
selling *Ireland's Issues*.
Their anxious faces press
to car windows.
In the space between
two languages,
their lips move.

2 *The Ice-Bird*

The thaw has abandoned it:
a bird of ice,
half-formed or half-dissolved
in a corner of the garden.
Flat out and faintly baleful,
for days it resists

the sun's best efforts.
The neighbour's cats stay clear.
More stubborn than road-kill,
winter's skin-and-bone,
it looks set to defy the season,
though we hug at the window,
though daffodils shake their spears.
Then, sadder than gravity
its miserable grey melt
into the earth.
We could do with some blackbirds now,
a few modest wrens,
taking their wings for granted.

3   The Shirt Factory

I love this innocent minute,
the frame full of girls
arriving on foot
from the side streets
off Limestone Road
years before the first bomb
and its thousand echoes.
Behind them the factory's
five red-brick storeys,
their local slab of industrial Belfast.
You'd swear it was built to last.
They flirt with the camera,
tuned to their working lives,
have a coy air of
secrets worth knowing:
the importance of thread, perhaps,
in setting the world to rights,
how the sewing on of collars
completes the creation.

4   *Derelict Building, Limestone Road*

Has matured for four decades into its ruin,
a Troubles installation that might be styled
'Flashpoint' or 'Intersection'. Five floors of angles
and silhouettes are all that's left
of its old lives as shirt factory and launderette.
Who would want to live here in no man's land,
where the closed circuit cameras, all neck and eyes,
rear from the pavement? But today the scaffolding
is in place, hoardings announce 'The Delaware Building',
an 'exciting development of luxury apartments'.
Balance itself and higher than anything,
the big crane is a peace mobile at the gable end.

5   *Storm, North Circular Road, 2 a.m.*

The night Hurricane Gordon
comes to die
on North Circular Road,
the roughed-up neighbourhood trees
keep bracing themselves,
the front gate, as I latch it,
is torn from my hands.
The rain makes no allowance,
there is no reason
for the wind to spare us.
Not fifty yards away,
a taxi idles
at the church railings,
lights full on, engine running.
No one gets in or out.
A white cat nobody guessed was there
bristles across the headlights,
then backs off hissing
into the whorl of the storm.
I retreat towards my own front door
before it slams in my face.

Northern Whig Bar

Jaroslav, Miroslav, Stanislav,
ill at ease
among the trendy drinkers.
The stone rings
that fixed them to the wall
at Party Headquarters
still sunk in their spines.
The stone eyeballs,
seasonally blind
to Prague springs and winters,
still dead in their sockets.
Jaroslav wrapped in a flag,
Miroslav's bullet-belt slung
like a bandoleer,
Stanislav's hand caressing a cannon.
But in this town
soldiers are out of date.
These, too, are decommissioned,
consigned for now
to a grey afterlife
modelling the old regime.
They inhabit a long present
where the past
grows longer daily.
In statueless streets
the cranes are hoisting
the city off its knees.
Immigrant workers
man the scaffolding,
their lives and ours
re-angled, re-aligned.

Small World

The field full of snow
so much a field full of snow
it needs a blackbird.

Tonight, in the smokeless zone, the drift
of fresh turf smoke –
a Christmas gift!

Hares on the grass patch
between the runways. Ears flat.
Ready for take-off.

Lost among your wet things
on the kitchen floor,
those two raindrop earrings.

Kneeling, we fill two buckets
to the brim. The well-
level does not change.

Tonight you will be late.
There is no moon. I leave
the gate on the latch.

Sensing a haiku
opportunity – those two
blackbirds, right on cue.

The longest day delights her –
daylight too
is out well past its bedtime.

The boiler growls in its out-
house. Winter gales
run wild on the mountain.

On the yard wall,
suddenly, a hooded crow.
Hard bastard. You can tell.

How relaxed she is,
that stray heifer
shitting her way through the graveyard.

Missing the fish's jump,
we have to make do
with the splash and its ripples.

Swept out as worthless,
the curled, perfect shavings
from the carpenter's bench.

That bald tyre too, snagged on the weir,
a bold strain
in the water music.

Above, the helicopter. Below,
in the restless streets,
its shadow.

The streets are empty.
Still I wait at the traffic lights
for the green man.

Pity to disturb him –
moth on the bedroom curtains,
sleeping alone.

Shadow lifts from the garden –
my neighbour's chimney
releasing the moon.

Again the valley fills
with a fox's cold bark
from the frost-white hills.

Cold as the Pole Star
the gush from the garden tap –
winter on my hands.

Moon-viewing from the back garden,
glass in hand –
the wine is liquid frost.

A funeral cortège
on the Westlink. Every-
body slows down.

Mud from my father's grave.
A whole week now, father,
since I cleaned my shoes.

Breathe on the bus window.
Wipe it clear. The world
as it is without you.

Touched once by the current
the pebble settles
for the next thousand years.

At last the Ice Age recedes.
In our garden, heels-up,
a dead blackbird.

Leaving Minnesota

I should have walked more in the snow
those muffled days
between the first dawn dazzle
and the muted glide
of headlights becoming tail lights
in a dusk
that was never darkness,
but snow-gleamed all night
in tyre-tracks, on packed pavements,
among dark winter trees.

But I stayed in and waited
while the bare lilac
knocked at the window
and blizzard or no blizzard
the sonorous planes
arrived and departed.

Yes, I, who knew I was leaving
from the day I arrived,
should have struck out at daylight
and left a trail
by White Bear Lake,
or printed a track at dusk
by the St Croix River and Minnehaha Falls
for the next wind to bury.

Where spring in Minnesota sends its slow
thaw through every trace of winter,
I should have walked more in the snow.

Colin Middleton, 'Lagan, Annadale' (1941)

There is something about this side of the river
that is the right side to be on. You know the trees
are set to survive the war, those walkers face
steadily into their lives, that child, you trust,
will grow to take peace for granted.

Praise to the enduring present, its gift today
a cocky tugboat puttering towards Drumbo,
or its home wharf, or autumn's furthest edge.
It holds the centre. Gracing its advance,
the wake fans out, lapping both shores at once.

The Telescope

Sunk in the battlements
of a restored, blood-soaked castle,
bolted to the stone,
it is angled to include
the city's parks, spires,
developments, industrial estates.
It invites us to look forward
and summons at last
a close-up of sky-bound waters,
impeccable hills.

But today a sudden
random dip to the edge
of a derelict street, holds,
magnified,
some traffic lights,
a police Land Rover,
a hole in a redbrick wall
from which explodes
a gang of anarchic children.
Bottles, stones, bolts,
blocks of wood,
a terracotta flowerpot,
some glass ashtrays
loosed with practised verve
against door and windscreen.
Passive, inscrutable, practised too,
the Land Rover sits out the attack,
reverses as though it might charge,
then swerves off
in a shower of lip-read fucks
and synchronised double-fingers.

Now they recycle their litter,
those handy bricks,
resilient ashtrays.
The future that hurtles towards them
hurtles towards us.
In the moments
we see it coming
it is ten times its size.
Like those monstrous meteor showers
we want to believe
could never collide with the Earth.

The Statues

Loveless, mirthless,
up to their plinths in snow,
they have been dragged here
from villages it seemed
they would dwarf forever.
Jettisoned at all angles,
they continue to strike
obsolete attitudes:
generals, commissars,
in a posed silence that suggests
definitive wisdom.
You want the snow to bury them
until all that shows
is a bald skullcap, say,
or the priapic tip
of a declamatory finger.
Then they can be exhumed
as harmless relics,
while the snow melts
and those cheerless provincial squares
blossom in fountains.

The Gate

I

There's a gate in the middle of the field.
It leads into the middle of the field and out of it.
We lean on the gate in the hedge that leads into the field
and stare at the gate in the middle.

II

Travellers point to the gate in the middle of the field.
They approach and investigate. They invest the gate
with mysterious purpose. They want to interrogate
whoever put it there. They admire a gate
that has gatecrashed the middle of a field.
Let all gates have such freedom, they think, bar none.

III

We swing on the thought of a gate in the middle of a field,
where it has no business, long after the gate has gone.
'Remember that gate?' we say and at night in our dreams
we head for the space in the middle.
We pass in file through the space in the middle of the field
and close, always, reverently, the gate behind us.

Avigliana

after Primo Levi

God help me, the man on whom the full moon,
the once-a-month full moon, is utterly wasted.
To hell with this town!
To hell with the fatuous moon –
as placid and unfazed
as though you were with me!

And that loud nightingale,
straight out of the Romantics –
I shooed him off
to the further side of the ditch.
How dare he sing
when I am so alone!

But the fireflies can stay,
sparking in scores along the footpath.
Not, Lucia, because their name reminds me of yours,
but for their gentle, cherishable presence
that short-circuits care.
If a day comes when we decide to part,
or a day when we want to marry,
I hope it will be a June day
with fireflies everywhere,
like this evening, when you are not here.

Some Spring Moons, North Circular Road

First the embarrassing moon,
so like nothing on earth
I bend my head at midnight,
closing the gates
on our threadbare planet.

Then the moon that seems to command
definitive utterance,
a clarifying take
so pure and simple no one can understand
it was not obvious.

Next the dizzying moon,
and the moon that has no time for us
but communes
with auto-banks and late-night taxis.
The unbeliever's moon,

shadowing the locked church,
the moon returned
off Cavehill tennis courts –
particular moon
becoming the universal.

Also the tracker moon,
and the moon that is keeping an eye,
and the absolute moon
that makes, on its night, unthinkable
a moonless sky.

But most the unblinking, ancient moon of spring,
making light of winter,
that hangs now in our windows,
spring-restored –
the moon in bloom, precarious and assured.

The Whooper Swan

for Michael Longley

When you croon your impression of a whooper swan,
at lunchtime, *sotto voce*, in Flannigan's Bar,
the notes are beyond language, you are living that sound
by tidal shallows a hundred miles away
in a season part-voiceless until the swans' return.
A moment's silence. I imagine each dolorous yomp
as a bid for the true pitch, as though it defers
to a lough's memory of winter or the last
death on an island, yet even in autumn lifts
a bronchial trump of resurrection.
When dawn was a soundless birth and sunset mimed
the idea of loss, the whooper happened in
with the vowel to suit October in these parts,
a tone that made somehow bearable the wind's
insistent dismissals, its miserly null-and-void.
Though earthbound, landlocked, I never lacked till now
the gift of a coastal childhood, or missed a life
edged with Atlantic: sea-self, sky-self, land-self
among the dunes in late autumn, balance restored
by the rich plaint, the vibrant ochone of the whooper swan.

The Builder

Anne Jane Ormsby 1913–1996

Even at fifty you were in demand,
three hayfields of your handiwork on show
each summer where your father's farm sloped
to the main road. So often we watched you step

into that rough circle. Your arms swept
round the prongs of dangerous pitchforks.
You seemed to embrace entire meadows,
patting them like aprons about your knees.

As you rose on your own foundation, people waved
from bus windows. The more you spread and trod,
above head-height, above hedge-height, the further we
had to step back not to lose sight of you.

You never looked like falling. Braced at the top,
you fielded the two hayropes, threw them back
nonchalantly between your legs
and prepared to return to the earth.

No memory now to match this: you gather your skirts
and slide with a girlish flourish
down the rick face,
land like a gymnast among our outstretched arms.

Selected titles from the OxfordPoets list

OxfordPoets, an imprint of Carcanet Press, celebrates the vitality and diversity of contemporary poetry in English.

Joseph Brodsky *Collected Poems In English*
For Brodsky, to be a poet was an absolute, a total necessity...scintillating deployment of language, and always tangential or odd ways of interpreting ideas, events or other literature. John Kinsella, OBSERVER

Carmen Bugan *Crossing the Carpathians*
To say these poems are beautiful is to risk underselling them. It is the specific nature of their beauty that matters, compounded as it is of dark experience, hope, magic, delight, generosity and love of language. George Szirtes

Greg Delanty *Collected Poems 1986–2006*
The fundamental tension that spurs Delanty's poetry crosses the domestic with the wayward, the retrospective with the prospective, and the result is a body of work that has grown steadily from book to book in depth, invention, and ambition. AGENDA

Jane Draycott *The Night Tree*
Hers is a scrupulous intelligence...Her searching curiosity and wonderful assurance make her an impeccable and central poetic intelligence. Penelope Shuttle, MANHATTAN REVIEW

Sasha Dugdale *The Estate*
Dugdale creates a spare, mythical tone that fits itself perfectly to the elemental Russian landscape in which much of her collection is set. GUARDIAN

Rebecca Elson *A Responsibility to Awe*
This is a wise and haunting volume, which I can't recommend too warmly. Boyd Tonkin, INDEPENDENT

Nigel Forde *A Map of the Territory*
Nigel Forde is a natural poet... It's obvious that both experience and thought make their impact on him in a rich mixture of imagery, rhythm and structure that enables them to be carried to us effortlessly. Arnold Wesker

Marilyn Hacker *Essays on Departure*
Everything is thrilling and true, fast and witty, deep and wise; her vitality is the pulse of life itself Derek Mahon

Anthony Hecht *Flight Among the Tombs*
Anthony Hecht's majestic development into a great poet has progressed across half-a-century. Flight Among the Tombs is his poignant and ironic masterpiece. Harold Bloom

Tim Kendall *Strange Land*
An intense and demanding collection. Its metaphysical honesty and its relevance demand our concentration. CHURCH TIMES

Jenny Lewis *Fathom*
The 'fathom' of Jenny Lewis's title resounds through her collection as noun and verb, implying both depth and the reckoning of it…Her poems, in fact, employ many of the techniques of painting, drawing readers in through the gleam of colours so intense and appealing as to be almost edible. GUARDIAN

Lucy Newlyn *Ginnel*
Don't doubt that this is very good poetry indeed…If you require a nostalgic hit of childhood and place, the ingredients which make this collection universal, it is here for you. THE LEEDS GUIDE

Robert Saxton *Manganese*
Intellectually persuasive, tough-minded and strikingly outspoken. This is an extremely well-read, cultured poet…He is also one heck of a craftsman, producing a dexterously sculpted poetry. ORBIS

Peter Scupham *Collected Poems*
He writes wonderfully about places, especially about English places…The sophistication of the technique which underpins every poem becomes clearer and clearer as you read further in this substantial, generous, distinguished volume. Peter Davidson, Books of the Year 2005, READYSTEADYBOOK.COM

Joe Sheerin *Elves in the Wainscotting*
The Irish poet Joe Sheerin's superb second collection… CITY LIFE

Penelope Shuttle *A Leaf Out of his Book*
Some of the poems are very funny…others divertingly offbeat or simply moving…there is a delight in the book as world, the world as book. TIMES LITERARY SUPPLEMENT

Charles Tomlinson *Cracks In the Universe*
Tomlinson is a unique voice in contemporary English poetry, and has been a satellite of excellence for the past 50 years. David Morley, GUARDIAN

Marina Tsvetaeva *Selected Poems,* **trans. Elaine Feinstein**
Marina Tsvetaeva was the first of the modern Russian poets whose greatness really came clear to me, thanks to these translations. Feinstein has performed the first, indispensable task of a great translator: she has captured a voice. THREEPENNY REVIEW

Chris Wallace-Crabbe *By and Large*
His allies are words, and he uses them with the care of a surgeon and the flair of a conjuror. Peter Porter